# Where's the Baby King?

BY KAREN KING

ILLUSTRATED BY
JANE COPE

STANDARD
PUBLISHING
Cincinnati, Ohio

ONE NIGHT LONG, LONG AGO, AN ANGEL
brought a message to some shepherds
on a hillside.

"Good news!" said the angel. "Today
the baby king is born in Bethlehem!
He is God's Son, who has come to save
all people. He will bring peace and joy
to the world."

A shepherd boy listened in wonder
as the angel told the shepherds they
would find the baby lying in a manger.

Then the shepherds hurried off,
leaving the boy to look after the sheep
while they went to see the baby king.

But the shepherd boy wanted to see this baby king too! So early the next morning, after the shepherds had come back to the fields and fallen asleep, the boy went off to Bethlehem by himself.

Soon he came to a house.
"Is the baby king here?" he called.

"The angel said he is God's Son," said the shepherd boy. "I must find him."

"I want to see this baby king too," said the man who owned the olive press.

So the shepherd boy and the man who owned the olive press went off to look for him.

Soon they came to another house. "Is the baby king here?" they called.

"The angel said he has come to save
all people," said the shepherd boy. "We
must find him."

"I want to see this baby king too,"
said the carpenter.

So the shepherd boy
and the man who owned the olive press
and the carpenter
all went off to look for him.

Soon they came to another house.
"Is the baby king here?" they called.

"The angel said he will bring peace
and joy to the world," said the shepherd
boy. "We must find him."

"I want to see this baby king too,"
said the spinner.

So the shepherd boy
and the man who owned the olive press
and the carpenter
and the spinner
all went off to look for him.

Soon they came to another house.
"Is the baby king here?" they called.

"The angel said he was born in
Bethlehem," said the shepherd boy. "We
must find him."

"I want to see this baby king too,"
said the potter.

So the shepherd boy
and the man who owned the olive press
and the carpenter
and the spinner
and the potter
all went off to look for him.

Soon they came to another house.
"Is the baby king here?" they called.

"The angel said he is lying in a manger," said the shepherd boy. "We must find him."

"I want to see this baby king too," said the shoemaker.

So the shepherd boy
and the man who owned the olive press
and the carpenter
and the spinner
and the potter
and the shoemaker
all went off to look for him.

Soon they all came to an inn.
"Is the baby king here?" they called.

"Who is this baby king?" asked the innkeeper's wife.

"God sent an angel to tell us about him," said the shepherd boy.

"He is God's Son," said the man who owned the olive press.

"He has come to save all people," said the carpenter.

"He will bring peace and joy to the world," said the spinner.

"He was born in Bethlehem," said the potter.

"And he is lying in a manger," said the shoemaker.

"Then let's look in the stable," said the innkeeper's wife. "A baby was born there last night."

So the innkeeper's wife went into the stable with the shepherd boy and
the man who owned the olive press
and the carpenter
and the spinner
and the potter
and the shoemaker
all following her.

"Is the baby king here?" they called.

The baby was lying in the manger.
His mother, Mary, smiled.
   Then the shepherd boy
         and the man who owned the olive press
         and the carpenter
         and the spinner
         and the potter
         and the shoemaker
         and the innkeeper's wife
knelt down together to worship Jesus,
God's Son, the baby king.

This edition published by The Standard Publishing Company,
8121 Hamilton Avenue, Cincinnati, Ohio 45231. A division of
Standex International Corporation.

Designed and produced by Tamarind Books in association with
SU Publishing 207-209 Queensway, Bletchley, Milton Keynes,
Bucks MK2 2EB.

Printed in China

ISBN 0-7847-0562-3